CURIOSI‘

of

EAST DEVON

Derrick Warren

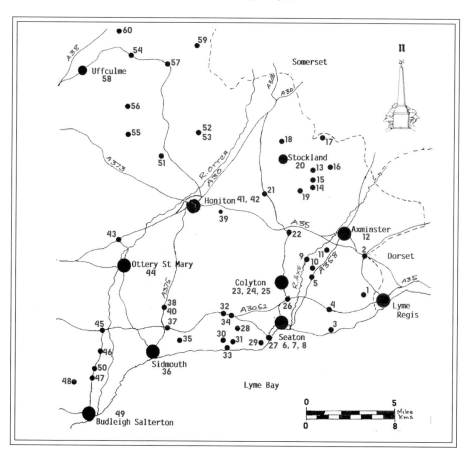

OTHER OBELISK PUBLICATIONS ABOUT EAST DEVON

The Great Little Exeter Book, *Chips Barber*
The Lost City of Exeter – Revisited, *Chips Barber*
The Ghosts of Exeter, *Sally & Chips Barber*
Beautiful Exeter, *Chips Barber*
Extraordinary Exmouth, *Harry Pascoe*
Entertaining Exmouth, *George Pridmore*
From Exmouth with Love, *George Pridmore*
From Budleigh Salterton with Love, *George Pridmore*
Around and About Seaton and Beer, *Chips Barber*
Along The Otter, *Chips Barber*
Cullompton Past and Present, *Jane Leonard*
Topsham Past and Present, *Chips Barber*
Sidmouth Past and Present, *Chips Barber*
Sidmouth in Colour, *Chips Barber*
Exmouth in Colour, *Chips Barber*
Pinhoe of Yesteryear Parts I and II, *Chips Barber*
Heavitree of Yesteryear, *Chips Barber*
Exploring Exeter, *Jean Maun*
Around the Churches of Exeter, *Walter Jacobson*
Around the Churches of East Devon, *Walter Jacobson*
Ten Family Walks in East Devon, *Sally & Chips Barber*
Walks on and around Woodbury Common, *Chips Barber*
Short Circular Walks in and around Sidmouth, *Chips Barber*

We have over 160 Devon-based titles. For a list of current books please write to
Obelisk Publications, 2 Church Hill, Pinhoe, Exeter, EX4 9ER or telephone (01392) 468556

Bibliography

Baring-Gould, S., *Devon*, 1899
Baring-Gould, S., *Devon Characters*, 1908
Bickley, F., *Where Dorset Meets Devon*, 1911
Blackmore, R. D., *Perlycross*, 1894
Chapman, G. M., *Dalwood*, 1983
Cooksey, A. J. A., *Admiralty Signal and Telegraph Stations*, 1974
Davidson, J., *The History of Newenham Abbey*, 1843
Devon C. C., *Devon's Heritage Buildings and Landscape*, 1982
Devon C. C., *Doorway to Devon*, 1978
Draycott, T. & Brian Clist, *Hemyock*, 1986
Evans, T. & Candida Lycett-Green, *English Cottages*, 1982
Grigson, D., *West Country*, 1951
Heath, S., *The South Devon and Dorset Coast*, 1910
Hoskins, W. G., *Old Devon*, 1966
Jones, J., *Rambles Round Chard with a Hammer*, 1860
Kelly, Allison, *Mrs Coade's Stone*, 1990
Medley, G. A., *A History of Sidbury*, 1980
Norway, A. H., *Highways and Byways in Devon and Cornwall*, 1911

Otter, R. A., Ed., *Civil Engineering History, Southern England*, 1994
Parker, D., *The West Country and the Sea*, 1980
The Penguin *Devon*, 1939
Pevsner, N., *The Buildings of England, South Devon*, 1952
Phillpotts, E., *My Devon Year*, 1904
Pulman, G., *The Book of the Axe*, 1875
Risdon, T., *Chorographical Description or Survey of Devon*, 1811
Shore, H. N., *Smuggling Days and Smuggling Ways*, 1892
St.Leger-Gordon, D., *Devonshire*, 1950
Thomas, D. St J., *Regional History of the Railways, The West Country*, 1960
Uffculme Archive Group, *Uffculme: A Peculiar Parish*, 1997
Ward Lock's Red Guide, *Lyme Regis and South Dorset*, 1914
Warren, C. H., *West Country*, 1938
Webber, D., *The Devon and Somerset Blackdown Hills*, 1976
Church Handbooks:
  St Winifred, Branscombe
  St Andrew, Colyton
  St Mary, Luppitt
  St Mary, Ottery St Mary
  St Giles, Sidbury

First published in 1999 by
Obelisk Publications, 2 Church Hill, Pinhoe, Exeter, Devon
Designed by Chips and Sally Barber
Printed in Great Britain by
The Devonshire Press Ltd, Torquay, Devon

©Derrick Warren/Obelisk Publications

Contents

Introduction

This book does not set out to be a guide, a history of the area or any sort of itinerary – it is merely an idiosyncratic collection of entirely unrelated facts and stories garnered during a lifetime's intimate knowledge of East Devon. Most can be seen and enjoyed by anyone but a few are private, whilst the few stories told are relatively little-known.

Map references are given for locations which might be slightly tricky to locate, but not for those which are private properties.

Eleanor Ludgate has provided the front cover illustration and the many original sketches. Eleanor, who trained at the Guildford School of Art, works from her gallery in Old Fore Street, Sidmouth, and is well known for her wildlife subjects as well as for her paintings of the area. Apart from pages 6 (middle and bottom), 8, 17 (top), 19 (bottom), 20 (bottom), 23 (top and middle), 24 (bottom) and 31 (top) which were supplied by Chips Barber, all but one of the other illustrations and photographs are from my own collection.

I should like to thank all those who have so kindly allowed me access to their properties and have talked so freely about what they so obviously love.

Dr Gilbert-Smith's seat

1. Cannington Viaduct (SY316924)

When the railway from Axminster to Lyme Regis opened in 1903 it was an engineering feat of some magnitude, for it had to climb nearly 500 feet in its first five miles, necessitating so many acute curves that only the Adams 4–4–2 radial-tank engines could negotiate them. These three special engines were known affectionately as 'Lyme Billies' after the well-known ability of Billy Goats to climb to the top of anything!

Before the line could descend to its terminus above Lyme Regis it had to cross a deep, wide valley at Cannington Farm, doing so on a 93-foot-high, ten-arch concrete viaduct. Although the line closed in 1965, the viaduct still stands as a magnificent memorial to the Railway Age.

2. Hunter's Lodge in the Axe Valley

It was once traditional amongst true Gypsies, on the death of the family matriarch, to burn her caravan. One of the last such rites was carried out near here in the mid 1950s. However, the local policeman who had to attend the fire, reported afterwards that everything of any value had been removed prior to the burning. This locality had long been favoured by Gypsies as a meeting place, probably because of the great yearly fair held on nearby Lambert's Castle since 1709, when a Charter was granted. This fair, held on the Wednesday before the Feast of John the Baptist (24 June), became noted for horse trading and the attendant horse races. Latterly only the horse races survived and these too ceased in 1947 when 'fixing' and shady dealing became so notorious that bookmakers would no longer attend!

The River Axe formed the boundary between the iron-age tribes of the Durotriges of Dorset and the Dumnonii of Devonshire. Both constantly carried out raids upon the other and, as a consequence, both constructed hill forts and camps (now commonly called castles), within whose earth ramparts their people and cattle could gather for safety. In East Devon the Durotriges' camps are those of Hawksdown Fort, Musbury Castle and Lambert's Castle. Those of the Dumnonii are Seaton Down Fort, Blackberry Castle, Berry Cliff Camp, Sidbury Castle, Peak Hill Camp, Farway Castle, Dumpton Hill Fort, Hembury Fort, Membury Castle and Stockland Great and Little Castles.

3. The Landslip between Seaton and Lyme

Many books have been written about this geological upheaval, but what is never mentioned is its peacefulness. Walking through the now overgrown wilderness of the Landslip on a still day

there is utter silence – except perhaps for the cry of a gull or peregrine. Silence, the most precious thing in this modern world.

4. Rousdon (SY294905)

The little hamlet of Downralph vanished completely with the building of Rousdon at the end of the nineteenth century. When Sir Henry William Peek (of Peek Frean biscuit fame) erected his neo-Elizabethan mansion on the edge of the cliffs, he rebuilt the whole hamlet, including the church, and gave it a new name. The mansion contains a great deal of Sicilian marble, the cargo of a boat wrecked, fortuitously, on the rocks below! The mansion became Allhallows School when it moved there from Honiton in 1937. By the side of the A3052 there is a stumpy, stone-capped, ashlar mile-post, also built by Peek.

5. The Fosse Way

Looking at a road map it becomes very apparent that Seaton must once have been a most important harbour, for why else should the Romans have constructed one of their great roads, the Fosse Way, leading to it before its finish at Exeter? The present A358 to Axminster and Chard closely follows the line of the Fosse Way until just after Tytherleigh, crossing the River Axe at Weycroft.

6. Seaton Harbour

It is difficult today to envisage Seaton as it must have been in Medieval times, with ships riding at anchor in the safe haven of the wide estuary of the River Axe and the busy quayside by St Gregory's Church. Gradually, however, the river's mouth was restricted by the encroaching pebble bank, the estuary silted up, the present marshes formed and Seaton returned to being a small fishing town until the 'seaside' holiday became the thing in the Victorian era.

7. The Toll Bridge at Seaton

Until just over a hundred years ago the first bridge over the River Axe was two miles upstream at Axe Bridge. The rough road from Axmouth to Axmouth Harbour was partially tidal and at very low tides it was possible for carts to ford the river a couple of hundred yards from its mouth, with pedestrians crossing by ferry from Axmouth Harbour.

The coming of the railway to Seaton in 1868 prompted a local landowner, Sir William Trevelyan, in 1875, to commission Philip Brennan to design and build a bridge across the river near the railway station.

Although Brennan was later to become an exponent of building with reinforced concrete, this bridge was constructed of mass concrete, with indented ornamentation to make it look as though it was of traditional stone construction. There are three spans, two of 30 feet, the centre one of 50 feet, and it was lit by gas lamps, two being at the centre mounted on the parapets. It was opened in 1877 and is the oldest mass concrete bridge in the country. The little single-storey tollhouse

(Sir William was not a philanthropist!), with its gently curving roof, is also built of concrete and it too is a very early example of the use of this material for housing. Tolls ceased to be charged in 1907 and the tidal road to Axmouth was 'elevated' to its present level in 1928 (no doubt the coming of the automobile had something to do with this!).

8. The Pebble Pickers of Axmouth Harbour

The pebble ridge, which had so effectively sealed up the Haven of the Axe Estuary, provided, after the Second World War, the material for an unusual industry – pebble picking. The pebbles were used in the preparation of the materials in paint making and in the production of 'slip', a liquid applied to pottery before firing to produce the glaze. Both these processes required a super-fine texture of the product and this was achieved by the pebbles acting as a grinding agent on the base materials in large revolving drums. However, the pebbles had to be of uniform size and roundness, and had to be individually picked up – not scooped with a shovel or mechanical digger

– hence the amusing name 'pebble pickers'. Another unusual use to which these pebbles were put was as a thick base for the finest bowling greens, for the pebbles provided superb drainage. They were even exported abroad, but the success of this little industry was its undoing, for in the 1960s it was thought that too many pebbles were being extracted, damaging the environment, so it was stopped.

9. The Stop Line of 1940

In 1940, had the Germans invaded this country west of a line from Seaton to Bridgwater, the Rivers Axe and Parrett were to have formed the basis of a defence line to prevent enemy forces penetrating eastwards. To reinforce these natural barriers, a great number of concrete gun emplacements, pillboxes and antitank barriers were constructed along the east bank of the River Axe. From Axmouth Harbour to Weycroft, north of Axminster, these can still be seen, stark reminders of those grim days, although in 1940 they would have been elaborately camouflaged. Along the whole line some 215 fortifications are still in place today.

10. Ashe House – Axe Valley

For over three hundred years Ashe House had been the home of the Drake family, although not of the same line as that of the famous Sir Francis. In the seventeenth century Elizabeth, one of twelve children of Sir John Drake, married a Dorsetshire gentleman and ardent Royalist, Winston Churchill. Churchill, having backed the wrong side, forfeited all his Dorset estates and had to retire to Ashe House and live with his wife's parents. On 24 May 1650, Elizabeth gave birth to a son, John. The house burnt down shortly afterwards and, although rebuilt by Sir John Drake (largely with stone from nearby Newenham Abbey [11]), little remains of the original except the chapel in which John Churchill was christened, and that, for many years, was used as a barn. John Churchill grew up to become the famous First Duke of Marlborough, victor at Blenheim, Ramillies, Oudenarde and Malplaquet. Today he is remembered for his beautiful home, Blenheim

Palace in Oxfordshire, and for his descendant and namesake of his father, the illustrious wartime leader, Sir Winston Churchill.

Ashe House is now hidden behind trees off the Musbury–Axminster road and is not accessible to the public but there is a splendid tomb of the Drake family in Musbury Church which can be seen.

11. Newenham Abbey (SY287974) – Axe Valley

The Order of Cistercians was founded in 1098 and by the thirteenth century they had 83 monasteries in England and Wales. Newenham Abbey was one of these and was situated on gently rising ground by the River Axe, just south of Axminster. At first it had only a small chapel but the grand Abbey Church was completed in 1280 and was dedicated to St Mary the Virgin. Its chief benefactors were Sir William and Sir Reginald Mohun of Ottery Mohun, with Bishop Bronescombe of Exeter giving £400, and the stone a gift from the quarries of Sir John de Staunton. The architect was Walter de Boreham and the design closely followed that of the Abbey Church of Salisbury, which was built a little earlier. Although smaller than Salisbury, the nave and choir being 180 feet long and the transept 152 feet wide, it was as elaborate and as beautiful. (In fact Alice de Mohun, the founders' mother, had paid for 12 years' stone for Salisbury.)

Cistercians professed to the Benedictine rules of devotion to God, poverty, chastity, fasting, prayer and labour. Newenham, however, became more secular and luxurious with a large establishment of both sexes! They owned extensive properties, farmed some 1700 acres and were prosperous merchants in wool and other products. The Dissolution of the Monasteries by King Henry VIII saw Newenham, in 1535, destroyed and her properties sold, and by 1690 "there was hardly left standing one stone upon another" (from John Prince's *The Worthies of Devon,* 1701; Prince was a scholar born at Newenham). Newenham was then plundered by the local landowners and townspeople for its stone, for, as Dr Johnson said, "walls supply stones more easily than quarries and palaces and temples will be destroyed to build stables and cottages". The great Abbey barn, 94 feet long and 30 feet wide, was spared because of its practical use, but when it burnt down in 1737 the destruction of Newenham was complete.

Throughout Britain the imposing ruins of the once great Abbeys can still be seen but at Newenham there is nothing – only a few walls still standing and those incorporated into modern farm buildings.

12. Axminster Carpets

Cosmo de Medici, Grand Duke of Tuscany, visiting Axminster in 1669, wrote that "it contains nothing remarkable except the parish church." He would not say that today for just under a hundred years later the name 'Axminster' was to become a household word. An Axminster clothier, Thomas Whitty, was in London and having seen a huge Turkey carpet "ornamented with large figures and without a seam" determined to make one like it. He succeeded and in 1755 produced one measuring 16 feet by 12 feet helped, it is said, "by the pliant fingers of little children".

This caused a sensation in the trade and his factory in Silver Street became famous, being visited in 1787 by Abigail Adams, wife of John Adams the American Republic's first Ambassador to the Court of St James (later to become the American Republic's second President). Two years later in 1789, King George III, with Queen Charlotte and all his family, made a special journey to visit and tour the factory. These visits resulted in Axminster carpets being laid in the White House, Windsor Castle and the Royal Pavilion, Brighton. The factory burnt down in 1828 but was rehoused in buildings, still standing but much altered, on the east side of The Square. Whitty's grandson, to the distress of the inhabitants, abandoned the business in the 1830s, the process going to a factory in Wilton, near Salisbury. One hundred years later a Kidderminster carpet manufacturer re-commenced weaving 'Axminster' carpets in a new factory outside the town and so revived an original industry.

13. Membury's Unusual Police House (ST278033)

The police house in this isolated village – it is not on the road to anywhere, which is fortunate, as its one street is picturesquely (and dangerously!) narrow – is not the usual 1920/30s police style. It is solidly built of stone, and over the door is a stone, handsomely carved with the Devon Constabulary Coat of Arms and the date 1873. Perhaps Membury was particularly lawless and warranted such special quarters!

14. The Quakers at Membury (ST272019)

To escape persecution many Quakers settled around this isolated village and held their Meetings in Lea Hill Farmhouse. Of course, they could not be buried in the parish churchyard and so had to have their own little burial ground. This was close by, high on Pomeroy's Hill, which commands stupendous views down the valley of the River Yarty to the sea and across to Membury Castle [2].

15. Membury's other Church (ST275025)

Pevsner says of St John's Church that it is Perpendicular in style with a taller and slimmer tower than is usual in Devon and that it is well worth a visit. He does not, however, mention Membury's little sister church at Rock, half a mile down the road. Built in 1821 by John Beasley, the twelve-year-old son of James Beasley, the village blacksmith, it is a miniature replica of St John's, being 12 feet 9 inches long, 3 feet 9 inches wide and 14 feet high to the top of the turreted tower. There are four gargoyles on the corners of the tower, the remains of a wrought-iron weather-vane and it once held a peal of five bells, which John is

reputed to have rung by himself – two with his hands, two with his feet and the fifth with his mouth! There is an inset stone inscribed JB AD MDCCCXXI. Once standing beside a rough track leading up the hill, it has since been incorporated in the rear garden of the nearby cottage, but although now much overgrown it can still be glimpsed from the road.

16. The 'Spy House' near Churchill (ST293024)

This true folly, in Brinscombe Lane above Churchill, was built at the end of the eighteenth century by a local landowner, Squire Davey, so that he could keep an eye on all his land (or, as the name given to it by his neighbours implied, to spy on them!). It was round, thatched and built of rough flint field stones and had iron grilles over the ground-floor windows. The upper 'spying' floor had large windows the whole way round and contained a huge circular table, built *in situ* at the same time as the tower. It was last used by the Home Guard during the Second World War, but was then, sadly, pulled down, leaving only a low stony mound to mark the spot.

17. Bewley Down's Wartime Secret (Blackdown Hills)

High on Bewley Down during the dark days of 1940–42, there was a very secret wireless station, officially known as an Auxiliary Units Operations Base (OB).

It was one of many such stations scattered across the country to provide information from behind enemy lines should there have been a successful German invasion and occupation of some of the country. The wireless 'net' that the Bewley Down station was on had its 'control' at Castle Neroche Farm.

At the bottom of a cottage garden were two back-to-back earth-closet privies, except that one of them was more than it seemed. In this one, the entire wooden seat, surround and bucket could be raised vertically on a steel frame by means of heavy counterweights on pulleys. When raised, this revealed a narrow shaft with a vertical ladder leading downwards. From the bottom a short and very low passage led into a concrete antechamber, about 5 feet by 4 feet and 6 feet high, with a 9-inch earthenware pipe in the ceiling curving away to five ventilators. Beyond the antechamber was a room 5 feet square constructed from curved sections of corrugated steel, the far wall being made of old railway sleepers. Against one side was a hinged wooden bench/bed and attached to the railway sleepers a hinged table. However, two of the sleepers to which the table was attached were hinged at the top and could swing forward and up, revealing a secret, similar sized, wireless room beyond. The whole was wired for electricity and connected to the cottage. The wireless aerials were concealed in the topmost branches of some old Scots pines in the nearby spinney, with their leads hidden under the rough bark of the trunks. The earth-closet could be raised by the person below on the receipt of a code (changed daily) given on an electric buzzer, the bell-push for which was on a post near the cottage, concealed by a climbing plant. It could also be opened from above, for one of the coat-hooks on the wall of the privy was hinged, and if pulled down would activate the counterweights and raise the earth-closet.

Such was the secrecy of this station's construction (and, of course, of all the others) that the Royal Engineer sappers were brought daily from their camp in completely closed trucks, ensuring that they could have no idea of the location. When completed, the station was 'manned' continuously by two ATS Subalterns who lived as civilians with the family at the cottage (the owner, incidentally, was a special constable).

There was a highly organised method of getting information (troop movements, unit descriptions, etc.) to the wireless station, involving a network of couriers, none of whom knew the identity of his (or her) fellow couriers. The messages were left in secret drops at the end of each stage and only the last knew the rough location of the station. Here, the message was put into a split-open tennis ball and dropped down a tube hidden in the roots of a tree in a hedge surrounding the spinney. This tube was inclined and led directly into the wireless room. Although all this now reads like a story from the Boys Own Paper, it was a deadly serious operation in preparation for an eventuality which happily never occurred. However, had it happened then few of these Auxiliary Unit members would have survived for long.

With the exception of the earth-closet itself and the wireless equipment, everything remains as it was in 1940, and is remembered, as a boy of 10, by the present owner, to whom I am indebted for this information. Although it is not quite as secret as it was it is still very private.

Bewley Down is often referred to by local people by its old name 'Billy Down' which itself is a corruption of an even older name 'Baaley Down', after the god Baal.

18. Fort Cottage (ST234060)

Near the parish boundary between Yarcombe and Stockland and at the very top of Rower Hill (689 feet) are the remains of Fort Cottage. This once thatched cottage was only small – two up and two down – but the crenellated front was built high and square with a small viewing platform, leaded and some 5 feet square, in the centre, and on the wall an oval plaque "DLD 1821".

It was built by the son of Major General Elliot Drake (later created Baron Heathfield for his heroic defence of Gibral-
tar during its siege of 1779–1783 when he was Governor General), of Sheafhayne Manor, on the southernmost edge of his Yarcombe estate, for one of his game keepers (presumably the viewing platform was to keep an eye out for poachers). During the early years of this century it was occu-pied by a family called Doble who had eleven children, and then dur-ing the Second World War by two elderly la-dies. There was no elec-tricity of course, and no piped water, only an 80-foot well and bucket and windlass. There was not even a made path to it up across the fields, let alone a track! It is aptly named, for the high crenellations of the little house stand out starkly against the sky on its lofty eminence.

Since this photograph was taken the old cot-tage has been demolished and, although rebuilt, has now become a 'Country Residence' with many more crenellations than the original!!

19. Beckford Bridge over the River Yarty (ST265014)

Where the lower road from Membury to Stockland crosses the River Yarty is one of the finest pack-horse bridges in Devon. This was once, of course, a ford and the narrow, steeply-arched, cobbled bridge enabled the pack horses, with their loads of wool or woollen cloth (for hundreds

of years the West Country was a famous producer of woollen cloth) to cross the often swollen river without their loads becoming wet.

20. A Stockland warning! (ST244046)

Until 1833 Stockland was an 'island' of Dorset completely surrounded by Devonshire and so was governed by Dorset's by-laws. An iron plaque on the stone parapet of the bridge over the River Yarty baldly states "DORSET. Any person wilfully INJURING any part of this COUNTY BRIDGE will be guilty of felony and upon conviction liable to be TRANS-PORTED FOR LIFE. By the Court T.Fooks. 7&8 Geo. A C30 S13".

21. Telegraph Cottage near Stockland (ST221009)

Telegraph Cottage stands beside the ridgeway road to the west of Stockland where it starts to descend to Wilmington. This was one of a chain of visual telegraph stations set up by the Admiralty in 1805, connecting Plymouth with London. Its neighbouring stations were St Cyres, Hill and Lambert's Castle, and it operated as follows. There were six shutters in two blocks of three, set side by side in a frame mounted on the roof of the building. The shutters were painted white with a black circle in the centre of each and were operated by ropes within the building, each letter of the alphabet having its own sequence of open or closed shutters. However, the shutters often could not be operated in high winds and in 1816 were replaced by a two-arm semaphore system designed by Sir Horace Popham. As both systems could only work effectively in clear weather one wonders what happened the rest of the time. In 1847 all these telegraph stations became redundant with the advent of the Electric Telegraph.

22. Shute Pillars (ST248984)

On an acute turn in the present road from Seaton Cross to Seaton Junction and about a mile from the handsome gatehouse to Shute House and Barton, there are two tall, stone pillars, surmounted by stone balls, one on each side of the road. These pillars were built long before the Turnpike road was constructed and so would have faced the old main Axminster–Honiton road, flanking what was in fact a country lane leading eventually to Colyton, but would have appeared to make rather a grand entrance to the Shute estate! No exact date can be given to the pillars but over the years they have received the attention of 'vandals' carving their initials and dates; the earliest on one is "TS 1743" and "HL 1711" on the other.

23. St Andrew's, Colyton

In the fifteenth century Colyton became a very prosperous woollen town and in the following century the wealthy merchants paid for an octagonal 'lantern' to be superimposed on to the top of St Andrew's square Norman tower. This form of church architecture, rare in England – the

most famous being St Botolph's in Boston, Lincolnshire ('The Boston Stump') – was popular in the Low Countries, with whom England traded extensively in woollen cloth. It is therefore likely that the Colyton merchants brought this idea of a 'lantern' back with them. The story that the 'lantern' was once illuminated to act as a beacon for ships entering Seaton Harbour is probably untrue, as it is not high enough to be seen out at sea.

Within the church, however, there are lights – glorious lights! Hanging over the nave are two great brass chandeliers, each holding 36 candles. They were bought for £82 in 1796 and these superb examples, probably the finest in the country, were almost certainly made in Bristol which was noted for this type of brassware.

24. Colyton House

Colyton House is bounded along Vicarage Street by a very high wall – over 20 feet – which has a rather unusual history. When, early in the twentieth century, the owner brought home his young and beautiful bride he became intensely jealous of her being seen walking in the grounds,

especially by a young man who lived in Berry House opposite. The jealous husband had the existing low wall raised to its present height, so that not even from the upper windows of Berry House could his garden be seen and thereby his wife was made safe from prying eyes! The young man, however, was not to be thwarted and had an extra floor built on to his house, enabling him once again to overlook the garden of Colyton House and see his inamorata. Unfortunately the story ends here as nothing is known of the final outcome. Perhaps the young man tired of just 'seeing her from afar', for the interior of that extra floor remained, for many years, incomplete and empty; and only recently, in 1996, was it made habitable.

The garden of Colyton House provides another sentimental story, but with no history to it at all. Under the great Holm Oak on the lawns of the house is a large, flat gravestone inscribed MAX MDCCCLXXIV (1874) followed by, in classical Greek capitals, a quotation taken from the Epistle to the Romans, chapter 8, verses 20 – 21. Its literal translation reads "In hope that the creature itself also shall be delivered". Very obviously Max was a dog that was much loved.

25. The Prince of Wales Fountain (SY245939)

In the centre of The Square at the top of Colyton's Market Street stands a handsome cast-iron Drinking Fountain (cast by the firm of Garton & King, Ironfounders, Exeter). It is decorated on two sides with the Prince of Wales Feathers and on the other two an inscription, which is given here without comment! "The surplus of a fund to commemorate the wedding of HRH The Prince of Wales [to Princess Alexandra of Denmark] during Lent, March 10 1863, has been devoted to the erection of this fountain by the patriotic Protestants of Colyton as a permanent memorial of that National Triumph and in vindication of their own loyalty by the vote of the Committee".

26. Cast-iron Stand-up, Colyford (SY254926)

The single-track branch railway from Seaton Junction to Seaton (opened in 1868) had a halt at Colyford, but after Beeching's Axe closed the line, the platform was removed so that passengers

could board the light trams which currently run over the Colyton–Seaton stretch of the line. Now stranded high and dry behind wire, on the original level of the old platform, is that once familiar feature on all small railway stations – a cast-iron urinal. This rare survivor stands as a stark reminder of the railway age, when everything was done for the convenience of travellers!

27. The Beer Conduits

When Judith Maria Waldron of Bovey House married John, Second Baron Rolle in 1778, she concerned herself with the welfare of the people who lived on her husband's estates.

Visiting Beer in 1780, she was distressed to see that the main source of drinking water for the village was the stream which flowed down the main street, used as it was as a convenient way of disposing night soil and the entrails of the fish gutted by the fishermen. Lady Rolle had two stone Conduits built across the stream, each with a spout from which gushed a constant flow of pure water piped from a spring at the head of the village.

The name 'conduit', besides being applied to a channel to carry water, was also used as a name for a stand or pillar from which there was a constant flow of water.

28. The Man Wheel at Bovey House, near Beer (SY208903)

This sixteenth century home of the Waldron family, later passed by marriage to the Lords Rolle, is now a very beautiful small hotel. An interesting feature is the well which once supplied the house. It is 130 feet deep and the huge bucket is drawn up by a man wheel, 14 feet in diameter. This is a treadmill – where the wheel was turned by a person or animal walking around the wheel's inner face. (The 300-feet-deep well at Carisbrooke Castle, on the Isle of Wight, was 'walked' by a donkey.) On one side of the well, 30 feet down, is a small chamber supposed to have been used, at a much later date, by smugglers as a hiding place for contraband. It is much more likely, however, to have been a priest's hiding hole. In the garden is a handsome lead water butt, highly decorated and with the date 1592.

29. Jack Rattenbury and Beer Caves (SY214893)

During the late eighteenth and early nineteenth centuries the occupation of smuggling was rife all along the South Coast of England and nowhere more so than in East Devon. The isolated, narrow valleys of Branscombe, Littlecombe, Weston and Salcombe, leading down to steeply shelving, shingle beaches, were ideal for this trade, with the haven of Beer and its fishing fleet as the headquarters. The lengths to which the preventive officers eventually went to try and control this coast can be seen in the line of coastguard cottages (now an hotel) at Branscombe and the ruins of similar ones at Weston.

Smugglers are often depicted in a romantic light but in reality they were violent and often murderous men engaged in a bloody duel with the riding officers. One, however, Jack (John) Rattenbury of Beer, was not of this violent mould, and became known as 'The Rob Roy of the West'. Born at Beer on 18 October 1778, he went to sea as a privateer at the age of 14, was press-ganged into the Navy when 16, escaped, and continued as a privateer – not very successfully – until he was 25. For the next 30 years he turned to smuggling for a living. Perhaps because he enjoyed the thrill and adventure involved and avoided the trade's violent excesses, he was never sought very actively by the law – only, to his disgust, by the Navy as a deserter – but he never made his fortune. He had married a local girl on 17 April 1801, and in between his privateering and smuggling ventures, he lived for a few years in Lyme Regis, where he was a contractor for Blue Lias (hydraulic) lime. When he was 58, and on hard times, John Lord Rolle granted him a pension of a shilling a week for his work in connection with the building and repair of the harbour at Sidmouth and the sea walls at Exmouth, for which Lord Rolle had been responsible. By 1837 his exploits had become legendary and in that year his autobiography, *Memoirs of a Smuggler*, was published in Sidmouth, although from the style of the prose it is doubtful if Jack actually wrote it. He was buried in an unmarked grave in the churchyard of St Gregory's, Seaton, on 28 April 1844.

Nowhere are Jack's 'romantic' adventures brought to life more evocatively than in Beer Caves, the vast underground quarries said to date from Roman times and from which much of the stone for Exeter Cathedral and many other local churches was hewn. It is here, tradition has it, that Jack stored his illicit brandy, tea and tobacco, and there is the usual smuggling story of a passage leading directly from the caves to the sea, which has since been searched for but has not been found – yet! However, I have a vivid childhood memory of being taken, by candlelight, through a passage in these caves and being lifted up to see the sea at its end, for there was a wall across the exit to prevent anyone falling down the steep cliff. The guide was an old man (this was in the late 1920s) who supplemented his income by carving and selling miniature stone bibles. The caves are now open to the public as a summer attraction and in the winter to the bats, for it is a nationally important site where these delightful creatures hibernate.

30. St Winifred's Church, Branscombe

This charming little church, snuggled protectively in its beautiful valley, has a host of fascinating features. There is a rare three-decker pulpit where the lessons were read from the bottom deck, the prayers said from the middle and from the top was preached the sermon. No other sundial is known where a buttress acts as a gnomon (the pin of the dial) which, in this case, is on the south-east corner of the chancel. Its shadow falls on Roman numerals cut into the wall of the church, which read from six to eleven in the morning. It is early fourteenth century, contemporary with the building of the chancel.

Engraved on a stone set in the floor of the chancel is a sweetly touching epitaph for an infant, Anna Bartlett, who died in 1609:

Here lieth a blossom of the world's great tree
Who was as fair as buds of roses be.
She died an infant – Heaven was made for such.
Live like an infant, thou shalt have as much.

In the churchyard outside is a grim reminder of smuggling days. The tomb of John Hurley, an exciseman, records that he fell from the cliffs whilst trying to extinguish a signal fire, lit to guide in a smuggling boat out at sea (or was he pushed?).

31. Branscombe's Old Bakery (SY197887)

Many villages now boast of having an old smithy or cornmill, but few can claim an old bakehouse as well. Although now a teashop run by the National Trust, all the original features of this tiny, thatched village

bakery have been retained – even down to the Vitbe and Hovis bread tins! It was still being worked as late as 1980.

32. Dr Gilbert-Smith's Seat (SY195911)

How many people driving along the A3052 between Colyford and Sidford have noticed, about half a mile east of the Three Horseshoes Inn, a semicircular stone seat, which was erected to the memory of Dr Thomas Gilbert-Smith?

It is not unusual for seats to be placed in remembrance of friends or relatives, but what makes this one unique is the inscription, which reads: "On this spot, at half past nine o'clock, after watching the glorious sunset of August Third, 1904, Thomas Gilbert-Smith, MD, FRCS, fell dead from his bicycle. Thunder and lightning immediately followed. Thus closed a noble life spent in the service of his fellow men. He never turned his back on duty but faithful to his motto 'Dare and Do' remained undaunted to the end." The plaque which carries this inscription replaces an earlier one which also showed the profile of Dr Gilbert-Smith and another picture of him by his bicycle, dressed in Norfolk jacket and knickerbockers. These gun-metal plaques were stolen in 1981.

33. Early Potatoes at Branscombe

For many years Branscombe was well-known, if not famous, for its very early potatoes. These were grown by the fishermen on the sheltered, level 'slips' all along the cliffs as far as Weston Mouth; as these 'slips' were only accessible by steep paths, donkeys with wicker panniers were used to carry the potatoes and the seaweed, which was used as a rich manure. They were last grown on any scale at Weston in the 1930s and now many of these level areas have been taken over by holiday chalets or simply overgrown by scrub.

34. The Hangman's Stone, near Beer (SY202909)

Where the most easterly lane to Branscombe joins the A3052, there is a large natural boulder known as the Hangman's Stone. The story has it that a thief, with a stolen sheep on the end of a

halter, rested on the stone; the sheep, in its frantic effort to escape, entangled the rope around the thief's neck and so strangled him! This explains the name but not the stone itself. When this main road was but a rough, unfenced trackway across wild heathland, the stone would have told travellers where to turn off for Branscombe. All over the country many such turnings and crossroads have similar boulders.

35. The Salcombe Regis Thorn (SY148891)

Where the lane leading down to Salcombe Regis turns off from the lane running along the top of the hill, there is a triangular piece of ground in which there is an inscribed stone and a thorn tree. The stone was erected in 1939 by Vaughan Cornish and Christopher Tomkinson, Trustees of the Thorn Estate, and reads: "A thorn tree has been maintained here since Saxon times when it marked the boundary between the cultivated field of the combe and the open common of the hill. It has given its name to the adjacent house, part of which is pre-Reformation, where the manor court was held, and to the surrounding farm". On moorland and other waste ground the thorn tree, because of its longevity and resistance to storm, was often used as a boundary marker, although it is more often only the name that has survived. In this case, of course, the tree would have been replaced, probably many times. The little brick building about a quarter of a mile to the east of the thorn is not, despite it appearance, a lock-up(!) but a well house and throw pump (the iron-barred gate is a later addition). It was erected in 1884 in memory of the Rev.T. Anderson Moorshead, Vicar of St Mary & St Peter, Salcombe Regis. The well is now 126 feet 9 inches deep, having had to be deepened in 1892 following a severe drought.

36. Crossing the Sid

There are far too many handsome and pictur-esque buildings in Sidmouth to single out any one – they have, in any case, all been described, photographed and eulogised over many times before. In the last half a mile of its journey, before it struggles through the pebbles to the sea, the little River Sid is crossed in three interesting and vastly different ways. On the road in from Seaton there is the old Turnpike bridge with its attendant early nineteenth century, single-storey, porticoed little tollhouse, and close by, but now across the driveway into the Byes, is the iron toll gate. Within sight of the sea, walkers can cross dry shod onto the steep coastal path to Salcombe Regis via the Alma Bridge. This was erected in 1855, at a cost of £70, to commemorate the Crimean battle of that name. This footbridge was rebuilt in 1900. Midway between these two, connecting Mill Street and Millford Road, is one of the few remaining fords in Devon, where anyone not old enough to remember this once commonplace way of crossing a stream – 'a water-splash' – can experience the anticipation of having the horse gib or the engine stall!

37. The Salt Bridge, Sidford (SY137899)

Where the main A3052 road now crosses the little River Sid at the bottom of the village, the twin parapets of the old packhorse bridge have been incorporated into the modern road bridge. When this was a ford the packhorse bridge was built to serve the salt trade (in Medieval times the evaporating of seawater from salt pans was an important aspect of this coast's economy). Further evidence of this is nearby in the name of a house – the Salt House, now an hotel and renamed the Salty Monk.

38. The Powder Room at St Giles Church, Sidbury

The Powder Room above the south porch of St Giles Church has nothing to do with its

modern American namesake! Long before the Home Guard or the County Militia were formed, every town and village had to provide a 'muster' of men to help defend the locality or county in time of trouble. Their arms, be they pike or musket, were usually kept at a central place, often the church, to be distributed in an emergency. At Sidbury it was in this room above the porch that the muskets and powder were kept in readiness.

39. Bishop Coplestone's Folly (ST183004)

This tower, together with a row of cottages, was built between 1842 and 1847 by the Bishop of Llandaff, Wales, the Very Rev. Edward Coplestone, who lived in the house nearby, to provide work for the great number of unemployed in the area. It is 70 feet high to the viewing platform, 80 feet to the cupola, both of which are leaded and surrounded by wrought-iron railings, and 100 feet to top of the weather vane. The first three floors are reached by a circular stone staircase in the SW corner and the last two by wooden steps. (In the early 1900s a water tank was installed on the fourth floor, leading to the local belief that the tower was built for that sole purpose.) The name Bishop Coplestone's Folly stemmed from the after-dinner story that the good Bishop was fond of telling – that he built the tower so that he could keep his eye on his Diocese in Wales!

40. Witch Scratching at Sidbury

In 1924 this village was the scene of what was probably the last case of witch scratching in this country. It was reported in the *Evening News* by a Mr Britten, who tells the story of this strange event which befell a friend of his. This man was cycling through the village when he was stopped by a gang of local lads. He dismounted from his bicycle and then, much to his surprise, the ringleader pushed a pin into one of his legs chanting, as far as he could remember the exact words, "Prickee wi' a pin and draw his blood an' ee can't hurt ee". Having done this 'witch scratching' the group were perfectly polite towards the stranger!

41. Copper Castle (ST171004)

On the west side of the A35 coming down into Honiton is Copper Castle. This is an old, crenellated tollhouse of the Honiton Trust c.1800. It is not only its name which is unusual; it has

also retained its original iron gates which once crossed the road although, the road having been considerably widened, the gates can no longer span the road but stand open on each side.

42. Leper Hospital (ST152001)

On the Exeter road out of Honiton, just beyond the turning to Sidmouth, are a pair of charming old thatched cottages, one on each side of the road. These were the almshouses and

next to them, now used as a church by the Assemblies of God, is the little Hospital of St Margaret, founded in the fourteenth century for the comfort and curing of lepers.

43. Patteson's Cross (SY096976)

This 20 foot high brick column, surmounted by a stone cross, stands in a grass triangle beside the busy A30 where it is crossed by the Ottery–Feniton road. It was erected to the memory of John Coleridge Patteson, Bishop of Melanesia, who, incidentally, was a cousin of the poet Samuel Taylor Coleridge. The inscription on the south side reads: "In memory of John Coleridge Patteson DD, born in London 1 April 1827. Killed at Nakapu, near the Island of Santa Cruz Sept 20 1871. Together with both his fellow workers for our Lord The Rev. Joseph Atkin, and Stephen Taroaniara, in vengeance for wrongs suffered at the hands of Europeans by savage men whom he had loved and for whose sake he gave up home and country and friends dearer than his life". At the very top of the pillar, just below the cross, are the directional names of four towns – Exeter, Honiton, Ottery and Feniton. The really odd thing about these names is that they are placed to tell the traveller where he has come from, not which way to go!

44. St Mary of Ottery

With the exception of Exeter Cathedral, this is arguably the finest ecclesiastical building in Devon – a cathedral in miniature. Unfortunately, as with so many other churches, much of its beautiful decoration and stained glass was destroyed and many of its effigies were defaced in the savagery of the Dissolution and during the Civil War (1642–1646) when General Fairfax occupied Ottery. This in no way detracts from the splendour of the fabric of St Mary of Ottery, and one fine ornament which did survive, possibly because it was of practical use, was the astronomical clock. Made between 1327 and 1369, when the earth was still thought to be the centre of the universe, the theory propounded by Ptolemy, it has a square face with an outer circle showing the 24 hour day in Roman numerals, with the hour being indicated by a golden sun which moves within the circle. The inner circle has thirty discs with Arabic numerals, with a star moving round to show the age of the moon. Within this circle is a black and white orb which revolves on its own axis to show the phases of the moon, travelling round the circle once in every 24 hours. There are three other similar clocks in the West Country – at Exeter, Wells and Wimborne Minster – but this is the only one worked by its largely original mechanism and is one of the oldest surviving mechanical clocks in the country.

Another, and much more visible, object also survived Fairfax's attention – just! This is the great copper 'whistling' weather cock on the top of the spire, so called because it has two tubes inserted into its body which moan in the wind. When Fairfax was in Ottery the weather cock was used by his men as a target for musket practice, with several balls piercing the tail. Some years ago the cock was taken down for renovation and was given a new tail, the original 'hol(e)y' tail being now on display under glass within the church.

45. Thatched Tollhouse, Newton Poppleford (SY079896)

Newton Poppleford (what an idyllic rural scene the name Poppleford conjures up, 'popple' meaning water tumbling and rippling) can boast the oldest tollhouse in Devon, built in 1758 for the Exeter Trust. The little single-storey thatched building is hard by the roadside at the western end of the village.

46. Water Tap, Colaton Raleigh (SY077875)

Nearly a hundred years had to elapse after Julia Rolle's gift of pure water to the villagers of Beer [27] before it was recognised that there was a direct connection between polluted drinking water and diseases such as cholera. It was more often the landed gentry who became aware of this, and many provided a pure water supply for their tenants. A descendant of Julia Rolle's husband was no exception, as this inscription by a water tap in the village testifies: "1887. This tap, with seven others, was erected as a memorial of the Jubilee of HM Queen Victoria for the benefit of the present and future inhabitants of Colaton Raleigh. The mains were provided by the Hon. Mark Rolle at a cost of £300 and the taps by the inhabitants at a cost of £12. God Save The Queen." The Hon. Mark Rolle obviously thought a little self-help was a good thing, for a similar inscription in the nearby and slightly larger village of East Budleigh records that its inhabitants also had to pay a proportion – £23!

47. The Scripture Stone or Brick Cross near East Budleigh (SY071852)

Where the lane for Otterton leaves the main road at Otterton Cross there stands a tall brick pillar surmounted by a stone cross. It is very similar in appearance to Bishop Patteson's Cross [43] and it also tells the traveller where he has been. The great differences are in the date (this was built in 1743) and in the inscriptions, for here the four sides of the pillar bear very apt quotations from the Scriptures – hence its name: "Make us go in the paths of Thy Commandments for therein is my desire"; "O that our ways were made so direct that we might keep thy Statutes"; "O hold Thou up our going in Thy paths that our feet shall slip not"; and "Her ways are ways of pleasantness and all her paths are peace".

An eighteenth century moral Highway Code!

48. East Budleigh – Sir Walter Raleigh's Birthplace (SY050851)

When Walter Raleigh, of Farwell, near Cornwood, married Joan Drake of Exmouth, he purchased the large farm of Hayes Barton at East Budleigh, so that his wife could be near her family. It was also conveniently close to his manors at Withycome Raleigh and Colaton Raleigh. It was here at Hayes Barton in 1552 that Joan gave birth to a son who was to become the great Sir Walter Raleigh and of whom James Thomson (1700–1748), poet and author of 'Rule, Britannia', was to say much later on Raleigh's *History of the World*, written when Raleigh was imprisoned in the Tower:

In Raleigh mark, then, every glory mixed,
Whose breast with all
The sage, the patriot, and the hero burned.
His mind
Explored the vast extent of ages past,
And with his prison hours enriched the world.

The long, thatched, two-storey farmhouse of Hayes Barton, with its gables and projecting porch, remains today much as it was in the sixteenth century, and although it is not open to the public, it can be clearly seen from Hayes Lane.

49. Budleigh Salterton's Famous Boy

Although Budleigh Salterton remains a charming seaside watering place it is also well known

as the setting for the famous painting 'The Boyhood of Raleigh' by Sir John Millais (1829 – 1896) in 1870. This depicts the young Raleigh listening with rapt attention to some daring tale of the sea told to him by an old sea salt. The low, curving wall by which the seaman is sitting is still there today, just where the promenade along the top of the pebble bank joins the town.

50. Bicton Gardens and Eleanor Coade

Eleanor Coade is one of the West Country's most eminent, although little-known, daughters. She was born in Exeter in 1733 and had a summer residence, 'Belvedere', at Lyme Regis, but lived mostly in London at her factory in Lambeth. Under her personal supervision the small works and studio produced superb statuary and building ornamentations in 'Coadestone', a highly weather-resistant ceramic stoneware. These were used by all the famous architects of the day, from Robert Adam to Sir John Soane, and can be seen at all the Great Houses of England and throughout London.

Here in East Devon, so close to Eleanor's roots, it is only at Bicton that any examples of her work can be seen. In niches on either side of the orangeries, looking down over the beautiful Italianate garden, are the busts of Lord Horatio Nelson and Sir Walter Raleigh, and high under the apex of the roof is the Duke of Wellington. Today they look as perfect as when they were cast some 170 years ago, and they bear witness to Eleanor's skill and to the durability of her invention, Coadestone. She died in 1821.

51. Wolford Chapel near Honiton (ST137052)

All along the road from Honiton towards Dunkeswell are signs, emblazoned with a maple leaf, directing visitors to Wolford Chapel – signs as prominent as those for any major national monument. Finally the visitors will find themselves in a narrow, moss-grown lane, at the end of which is a rather unprepossessing little church, beside which is a tall flagstaff flying the flag of the State of Ontario, Canada.

The fact is, this *is* a little bit of Ontario, for it was given to that state in 1966 by the then owner of Wolford House, Sir Geoffrey Harmsworth. But why was it given and, from a quick glance at the visitors' book in the church, why is it such a place of pilgrimage for Canadians?

Wolford House was once the home of General John Graves Simcoe (1752 – 1806) and the little church was built by him in 1800. General Simcoe joined the army when he was eighteen and during the American War of Independence commanded the First American Regiment (Queen's

Rangers). In 1791 he was appointed the first Lieutenant General of the newly formed Province of Upper Canada and during his energetic administration he improved communications, encouraged immigration and founded the town of York, which later became Toronto. He went on to become Governor and Military Commander of St Domingo, commanded the Western Military Division when England was threatened by French invasion during 1801 to 1804 and in 1806 was appointed Commander-in-Chief of India. However, he died before he could take up the post and was buried in this church, having bought the Wolford Estate in 1784.

His wife Elizabeth, and his six daughters (all unmarried) Eliza, Charlotte, Henrietta, Caroline, Sophie and Katherine, are all buried here. Another daughter, also Katherine, and a son, John Cornwall, died in infancy in Canada. His other son, Francis Gwillian, "died in the breach at the siege of Badajoz, April 6 1812 in the 21st year of his life". Over the pulpit, General Simcoe's life is aptly summed up. "As for me and my house we will serve the Lord. XXIV 15 MDCCCII." The chapel is administered by the John Graves Simcoe Memorial Foundation, Ontario.

52. 'Luppitt Harbour' (ST173064)

During the latter half of the nineteenth century and the beginning of the twentieth, Luppitt had two football teams – 'the Sailors' and 'the Dockers' – the members of the respective teams living on either side of the brook, the River Love, which flows down the valley. Until quite recently, where this brook crossed the road leading up to the church, there was a very wide, shallow ford. This was known locally as 'Luppitt Harbour', with the male resident of the cottage directly east of the ford having the honorary title of 'Harbourmaster'. The last 'Harbourmaster', Tim Davey, who died in 1982, had an old postcard of about 1905, coloured in the style of that era, which was a photograph of this wide ford but with a much-reduced photograph of a battleship superimposed on the water! The whereabouts of the postcard is now unknown but I was shown it in 1960 by the 'Harbourmaster'.

Surprisingly, all the above nonsense has a basis of fact and makes a fascinating example of how folk stories originate.

During the Civil War of 1642–1646 between the Royalists under Charles I and the Parliamentarians under Cromwell, the Parliamentarians had a small army camped on Hartridge, an area of high, level ground to the east of Luppitt. The Royalists in the area were heavily outnumbered and called for reinforcements from their nearest garrison, which was at Exeter. However, no soldiers could be spared but a small contingent of sailors was dispatched from Topsham. The story has it that they sailed up the brook from Budleigh Salterton! But anyway, they scaled the steep, wooded slope of the hill, which to this day is named Luppitt Shore, and helped win the day for the Royalists.

53. The 'Pagan' Font at St Mary's Church, Luppitt

The Norman font in this little village church is even more worthy of note than the beautiful wagon-roofs or the impressive gargoyles on the outside of the north wall. The font is square and

the carvings on its four sides are barbaric in their representation. Pevsner describes them as "centaur fighting two dragons, two men fighting each other with nail-shaped big clubs, a group of dachshund-like animals and a tree with dishevelled foliage (tree of life treated by an exceptionally unconventional carver?)". Another description says "curious grotesques and a pagan centaur (note especially the priapus, which at first sight might be taken for a tail). It is possible that the image of the demon swallowing the top of the human head is a symbolic representation of demonic possession, the idea being that the demon is in charge of the thinking of the human being it is attacking." All writers, however, attest the pagan origins of the carvings and the assimilation of the old beliefs into the Christian religion.

In Greek mythology, Priapus was the son of Dionysus and Aphrodite, the god of reproductive power and fertility, the protector of shepherds, fishermen and farmers. He was later regarded as the chief deity of lasciviousness and obscenity and the phallus was his attribute.

According to one authority the name Luppitt stems from 'Love-pit', after a religious order (!) that once lived in the valley but was disbanded by the Mohuns of Ottery Mohun some time before the thirteenth century.

54. Culmstock's High Yew

R. D. Blackmore (b.1825), the author of *Lorna Doone*, grew up in Culmstock and set his less well-known romantic novel, *Perlycross*, in the area. In this he mentions the little yew tree growing out of the masonry at the top of All Saints Church tower. It still grows in that precarious position and Blackmore's childhood memory therefore puts the age of this little yew at 200 years at least!

55. The Whetstone Mines (ST099083 – ST105064)

Just under the steep escarpment which extends from Blackborough towards Broadhembury, is a trackway. On the higher, east side of this can still be seen the depressions which mark the dozens of collapsed adits, or tunnels, which were driven into the hillside to extract the special sandstone which, when shaped, was used for whetstones. In the days when crops were cut by either a scythe or a sickle, the whetstone, used to sharpen the blades, was an important and valuable piece of equipment. The mines were worked for close on 200 years, mainly by miners from Cornwall, who took them to the market for this trade at Exeter. They did not finally close until the end of the nineteenth century. Under the promontory on this escarpment, at the end of the present gliding club's ground, is an area of broken ground with many circular depressions. These, however, have nothing to do with the whetstone mines but are the remains of bell-pits, where, from Roman to early Medieval times, iron ore was mined to support the local iron smelting trade.

56. Garnsey's Tower at Blackborough (ST102095)

Hidden in the woods above Blackborough is the large mound that is all that remains of Garnsey's Tower. It was built by two brothers, John and Thomas Garnsey of Bodmiscombe Manor, about the turn of the eighteenth and nineteenth centuries, as a folly or look-out. It was 12 feet in diameter and some 35 feet high and from its top a 360 degree view could be obtained for over 40 miles.

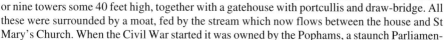

57. Hemyock Castle

East Devon abounds with 'Castles' and 'Forts', but most are relics of the iron-age hill-camps of the Durotriges and Dumnonii; Hemyock Castle, however, is an exception.

In 1381 William Asthorp was given permission to fortify his Manor House (for that is all it ever was – a fortified house) which he surrounded by a 5 feet thick, 18 feet high curtain wall and eight or nine towers some 40 feet high, together with a gatehouse with portcullis and draw-bridge. All these were surrounded by a moat, fed by the stream which now flows between the house and St Mary's Church. When the Civil War started it was owned by the Pophams, a staunch Parliamentary family, and was used as a prison for Royalists. In 1643 it was besieged by the Royalists, who eventually captured it and released some 200 prisoners. On the restoration of the monarchy in 1660, King Charles II ordered the 'castle' to be 'slighted'. As a result of this 'slighting' only fragments of the curtain wall and two towers remain, although the gatehouse is in a good state of preservation. This can be seen from the path which runs beside the stream.

Stocks are a fairly common village feature, but in the grounds of the Castle is that rarer form of punishment – a pillory.

58. The Shambles, Uffculme

Many towns such as Dartmouth, Totnes and Kingsbridge have their shambles – solidly built, open-fronted, colonnaded buildings where traders could set up their stalls to sell meat, fish and farm products. The Shambles in the centre of The Square at Uffculme is not like those at all – for it is only large enough for one stall and that was specifically for meat. It is a completely open timber-framed structure 13 feet by 9 feet, with a steeply-pitched, slate roof and carved barge-boards, built in the seventeenth century or earlier.

It became disused when a butcher opened a shop in the village but has now been found another use; it has been beautifully restored, and its counter replaced by a double wooden seat.

59. The Murderer's Stone (ST166145)

Far up the remote valley of the River Culm, near the charmingly named hamlet of Rosemary Lane, a neat cast-iron plate stands beside the road. It reads: "Wm Blackmore, Land Surveyor, of Clayhidon Mills, was murdered on this spot the 6th Day of February 1853 by George Sparks, of this parish, who was executed at Exeter for this horrid crime". The story behind this is prosaic enough. Blackmore went to collect money from a farmer, John Honeyball, and the transaction was seen by two of his men, George Sparks and Hitchcock. Sparks and Hitchcock went drinking that evening at the White Horse Inn at Bolham and again met Blackmore; at 1.00 a.m. they left together, laughing and talking amicably. However, after Hitchcock had gone his separate way, Sparks hit Blackmore with a heavy pair of tongs he had been carrying, killing him and taking the money. Sparks was arrested, tried and then, on a new scaffold, was executed at Exeter before a crowd of 12,000.

What makes this commemorative plate so unusual is that either the parish or Blackmore's friends and relatives felt the need, at no little cost, to remember the event in such a permanent manner. After all, murder for gain was not uncommon and was rarely commemorated so publicly.

60. Spiceland (ST082138)

The interiors of the Meeting Houses of the Society of Friends (Quakers) all follow the same pattern of simplicity, with their plain wood benches, the raised dais for the Elders and the complete absence of any form of decoration. Spiceland, built simply of stone and slate in 1815, is no exception, and with light flooding in through the round-headed windows, there is a great feel-ing of peace and tranquillity. All this is enhanced by its pastoral isolation for, with the exception of

the communicating cottage, there is no human habitation within sight or hearing. Although all are welcome to the Meetings it is not open at other times.